Directions for the priuate reading of the Scriptures wherein besides the number of chapters assigned to euery day, the order and drift of the whole Scriptures is methodically set downe (1618)

Nicholas Byfield

Directions for the priuate reading of the Scriptures wherein besides the number of chapters assigned to euery day, the order and drift of the whole Scriptures is methodically set downe
Byfield, Nicholas, 1579-1622.
[Edition statement:] The second edition.
The edition statement precedes the author statement on title page.
[24], 117, [3] p.
London : Printed by E. Griffin for N. Butter neere St. Austens gate, 1618.
STC (2nd ed.) / 4214
English
Reproduction of the original in the Bodleian Library

Early English Books Online (EEBO) Editions

Imagine holding history in your hands.

Now you can. Digitally preserved and previously accessible only through libraries as Early English Books Online, this rare material is now available in single print editions. Thousands of books written between 1475 and 1700 and ranging from religion to astronomy, medicine to music, can be delivered to your doorstep in individual volumes of high-quality historical reproductions.

We have been compiling these historic treasures for more than 70 years. Long before such a thing as "digital" even existed, ProQuest founder Eugene Power began the noble task of preserving the British Museum's collection on microfilm. He then sought out other rare and endangered titles, providing unparalleled access to these works and collaborating with the world's top academic institutions to make them widely available for the first time. This project furthers that original vision.

These texts have now made the full journey -- from their original printing-press versions available only in rare-book rooms to online library access to new single volumes made possible by the partnership between artifact preservation and modern printing technology. A portion of the proceeds from every book sold supports the libraries and institutions that made this collection possible, and that still work to preserve these invaluable treasures passed down through time.

This is history, traveling through time since the dawn of printing to your own personal library.

Initial Proquest EEBO Print Editions collections include:

Early Literature

This comprehensive collection begins with the famous Elizabethan Era that saw such literary giants as Chaucer, Shakespeare and Marlowe, as well as the introduction of the sonnet. Traveling through Jacobean and Restoration literature, the highlight of this series is the Pollard and Redgrave 1475-1640 selection of the rarest works from the English Renaissance.

Early Documents of World History

This collection combines early English perspectives on world history with documentation of Parliament records, royal decrees and military documents that reveal the delicate balance of Church and State in early English government. For social historians, almanacs and calendars offer insight into daily life of common citizens. This exhaustively complete series presents a thorough picture of history through the English Civil War.

Historical Almanacs

Historically, almanacs served a variety of purposes from the more practical, such as planting and harvesting crops and plotting nautical routes, to predicting the future through the movements of the stars. This collection provides a wide range of consecutive years of "almanacks" and calendars that depict a vast array of everyday life as it was several hundred years ago.

Early History of Astronomy & Space

Humankind has studied the skies for centuries, seeking to find our place in the universe. Some of the most important discoveries in the field of astronomy were made in these texts recorded by ancient stargazers, but almost as impactful were the perspectives of those who considered their discoveries to be heresy. Any independent astronomer will find this an invaluable collection of titles arguing the truth of the cosmic system.

Early History of Industry & Science

Acting as a kind of historical Wall Street, this collection of industry manuals and records explores the thriving industries of construction; textile, especially wool and linen; salt; livestock; and many more.

Early English Wit, Poetry & Satire

The power of literary device was never more in its prime than during this period of history, where a wide array of political and religious satire mocked the status quo and poetry called humankind to transcend the rigors of daily life through love, God or principle. This series comments on historical patterns of the human condition that are still visible today.

Early English Drama & Theatre

This collection needs no introduction, combining the works of some of the greatest canonical writers of all time, including many plays composed for royalty such as Queen Elizabeth I and King Edward VI. In addition, this series includes history and criticism of drama, as well as examinations of technique.

Early History of Travel & Geography

Offering a fascinating view into the perception of the world during the sixteenth and seventeenth centuries, this collection includes accounts of Columbus's discovery of the Americas and encompasses most of the Age of Discovery, during which Europeans and their descendants intensively explored and mapped the world. This series is a wealth of information from some the most groundbreaking explorers.

Early Fables & Fairy Tales

This series includes many translations, some illustrated, of some of the most well-known mythologies of today, including Aesop's Fables and English fairy tales, as well as many Greek, Latin and even Oriental parables and criticism and interpretation on the subject.

Early Documents of Language & Linguistics

The evolution of English and foreign languages is documented in these original texts studying and recording early philology from the study of a variety of languages including Greek, Latin and Chinese, as well as multilingual volumes, to current slang and obscure words. Translations from Latin, Hebrew and Aramaic, grammar treatises and even dictionaries and guides to translation make this collection rich in cultures from around the world.

Early History of the Law

With extensive collections of land tenure and business law "forms" in Great Britain, this is a comprehensive resource for all kinds of early English legal precedents from feudal to constitutional law, Jewish and Jesuit law, laws about public finance to food supply and forestry, and even "immoral conditions." An abundance of law dictionaries, philosophy and history and criticism completes this series.

Early History of Kings, Queens and Royalty

This collection includes debates on the divine right of kings, royal statutes and proclamations, and political ballads and songs as related to a number of English kings and queens, with notable concentrations on foreign rulers King Louis IX and King Louis XIV of France, and King Philip II of Spain. Writings on ancient rulers and royal tradition focus on Scottish and Roman kings, Cleopatra and the Biblical kings Nebuchadnezzar and Solomon.

Early History of Love, Marriage & Sex

Human relationships intrigued and baffled thinkers and writers well before the postmodern age of psychology and self-help. Now readers can access the insights and intricacies of Anglo-Saxon interactions in sex and love, marriage and politics, and the truth that lies somewhere in between action and thought.

Early History of Medicine, Health & Disease

This series includes fascinating studies on the human brain from as early as the 16th century, as well as early studies on the physiological effects of tobacco use. Anatomy texts, medical treatises and wound treatment are also discussed, revealing the exponential development of medical theory and practice over more than two hundred years.

Early History of Logic, Science and Math

The "hard sciences" developed exponentially during the 16th and 17th centuries, both relying upon centuries of tradition and adding to the foundation of modern application, as is evidenced by this extensive collection. This is a rich collection of practical mathematics as applied to business, carpentry and geography as well as explorations of mathematical instruments and arithmetic; logic and logicians such as Aristotle and Socrates; and a number of scientific disciplines from natural history to physics.

Early History of Military, War and Weaponry

Any professional or amateur student of war will thrill at the untold riches in this collection of war theory and practice in the early Western World. The Age of Discovery and Enlightenment was also a time of great political and religious unrest, revealed in accounts of conflicts such as the Wars of the Roses.

Early History of Food

This collection combines the commercial aspects of food handling, preservation and supply to the more specific aspects of canning and preserving, meat carving, brewing beer and even candy-making with fruits and flowers, with a large resource of cookery and recipe books. Not to be forgotten is a "the great eater of Kent," a study in food habits.

Early History of Religion

From the beginning of recorded history we have looked to the heavens for inspiration and guidance. In these early religious documents, sermons, and pamphlets, we see the spiritual impact on the lives of both royalty and the commoner. We also get insights into a clergy that was growing ever more powerful as a political force. This is one of the world's largest collections of religious works of this type, revealing much about our interpretation of the modern church and spirituality.

Early Social Customs

Social customs, human interaction and leisure are the driving force of any culture. These unique and quirky works give us a glimpse of interesting aspects of day-to-day life as it existed in an earlier time. With books on games, sports, traditions, festivals, and hobbies it is one of the most fascinating collections in the series.

The BiblioLife Network

This project was made possible in part by the BiblioLife Network (BLN), a project aimed at addressing some of the huge challenges facing book preservationists around the world. The BLN includes libraries, library networks, archives, subject matter experts, online communities and library service providers. We believe every book ever published should be available as a high-quality print reproduction; printed on-demand anywhere in the world. This insures the ongoing accessibility of the content and helps generate sustainable revenue for the libraries and organizations that work to preserve these important materials.

The following book is in the "public domain" and represents an authentic reproduction of the text as printed by the original publisher. While we have attempted to accurately maintain the integrity of the original work, there are sometimes problems with the original work or the micro-film from which the books were digitized. This can result in minor errors in reproduction. Possible imperfections include missing and blurred pages, poor pictures, markings and other reproduction issues beyond our control. Because this work is culturally important, we have made it available as part of our commitment to protecting, preserving, and promoting the world's literature.

GUIDE TO FOLD-OUTS MAPS and OVERSIZED IMAGES

The book you are reading was digitized from microfilm captured over the past thirty to forty years. Years after the creation of the original microfilm, the book was converted to digital files and made available in an online database.

In an online database, page images do not need to conform to the size restrictions found in a printed book. When converting these images back into a printed bound book, the page sizes are standardized in ways that maintain the detail of the original. For large images, such as fold-out maps, the original page image is split into two or more pages

Guidelines used to determine how to split the page image follows:

- Some images are split vertically; large images require vertical and horizontal splits.
- For horizontal splits, the content is split left to right.
- For vertical splits, the content is split from top to bottom.
- For both vertical and horizontal splits, the image is processed from top left to bottom right.

DIRECTIONS
for the priuate reading
of the Scriptures;

Wherein besides the number of Chapters assigned to every day, the order and drift of the whole SCRIPTVRES is methodically set downe:

And choice Rules (that shew how to read with profit) are likewise given:

The Vse whereof is shewed *in the Preface.*

The Second Edition.

By NICOLAS BIFEILD
Preacher of GODS word at
Isleworth in Middlesex.

LONDON
Printed by *E. Griffin* for *N. Butter*
neere S.t Austensgate. 1618.

To the noble Knight,
Sʳ HORRACE VERE,
Generall of the English-forces
in the *Low-countries.*

AND

To the most worthy Lady,
the Lady MARY VERE his
Wife, *my most respected and
religious Parishioners.*

Here are three things incite me, to Dedicate this little direction to your Lordship and my Lady:

A 2   The

The Epistle.

The first is to testifie hereby vnto the world my vnfained estimation of those sauing graces and the true religion that dwels in you both. The second is, to expresse hereby my great desire to shew my thankefulnesse, for the many fauours I haue receiued, but especially for all the incouragements wherewith I haue beene refreshed in obseruing your loue to my Ministerie,

Dedicatorie.

sterie, and care in your selues and your familie to shew the profit of it. The third is, because it pleased your Lordship and my Lady heretofore, to desire and accept directions of this kinde from me, in writing.

I haue beene the willinger to suffer this copy to come into publike view, because I haue beene vrged by many friends from diuers pla-

The Epistle

ces of late, to giue them Directions of this kind: and I haue long obserued that in the most places the godly that are vnlearned, are at a great want of a setled course herein. If it may please your Lordshippe and my Lady to afford this little worke, your acceptation and countenance, I shall be richly satisfied. My hope is that the Lord that hath as it were called for it by

the

Dedicatorie.

the request of many well disposed, will bee pleased to giue a blessing to it: if any thing be now wanting, by the intimation of my friends, I may make further supply in after Editions, if God will.

The Lord multiplie grace & ioy with righteousnesse and peace in both your hearts and liues, and prolong with increase your Lordships honour and good suc-

The Epistle

cesse in your militarie calling, in which you haue beene hitherto a speciall ornament to this Nation. I end and rest

Yours in the

seruice of my ministery

to be commanded,

N. BIFEILD.

The Preface.

THESE directions for reading the SCRIPTVRES *containe three things.* First *Analyticall tables, concerning the order of the whole* SCRIPTVRES, *and the seuerall bookes and Chapters gathered to this end, that the Reader might before hee reads, marke the drift of each booke and Chapter, and when hee hath read, might with singular ease and de-*

The Preface.

delight remember, what hee hath read. The second is a Calendar, shewing what number of chapters are to be reade euery day, that so the whole Bible might bee read ouer in a yeere. The number of Chapters, while you are reading the olde Testament is for the most part three a day, and when you come to the new Testament, it is but two: Sometimes where the matter is Historicall, or Typicall, or the chapters short, I haue set downe a greater number. The third thing is the Rules for obseruation of profitable things in reading. Many complaine of their not profiting in reading, and some weake Christians afflict their hearts

The Preface.

hearts maruellously with griefe and feare, because they cannot read with more comfort and profit, when the fault is not in their affection to the word, so much as in their want of direction for their reading.

Concerning these Rules I consider both the matter, and the maner of vsing them. For the matter, hee that comes to read the Scriptures, should especially set himselfe to obserue two things: First the most needfull places to enlarge his owne knowledge, and further his owne growth in the true grace of God. Secondly such places, as might warrant his practise in the things, the world vsually cauills at and reprocheth

The Preface.

eth his profession for: as if hee did not what were necessary to doe. There are some things in all places obiected against the godly. Now it is a thing of admirable use in our reading to gather vnder the seuerall heads such places, as may establish our hearts with abundance of assurance, that we do nothing out of precisenesse and curiositie in those things: but meerly at the commandement of God. And the Scriptures are so apparant, and easie to bee discerned, and so many in number, that the simplest Reader may gather great store of testimonies.

Now for the first of these, that is, such places as might most profit me in my particuler reading:

The Preface.

ding: *I would bring this minde to the Scriptures. (I will but giue a tast here.)*

First it were a thing of admirable vse all my life long, if I did set downe all the places of Scripture, that in the reading I finde sensible comfort and rauishing of heart in: It may be in the whole Bible I may finde 20. 40. 50. &c. of such places, as I was sure in the reading did wonderfully fill my heart with secret refreshing, and sensible ioy: Now these places so noted, not onely serue for present vse, but while I liue, in any distresse, I may haue recourse to these, as so many wells of ioy, and if in my griefe one, or two, or tenne of them did not comfort mee:

yet.

The Preface.

yet a thousand to one some of them will haue spirit and life in them to refresh me againe in any sorrowes: Besides, it maruellously establisheth my faith, when I remember, in how many distinct places of Scripture the Lord was pleased to comfort me in particular. This is one thing now wee should observe.

Secondly would it not be exceeding profitable; If I did note all the places of scripture which in reading of them did sensibly smite my heart, and reprooue some fault in mee, so as I felt my heart troubled within mee? Certainely by that time I had gone through the Scriptures, I should see the Anatomy of my
corrup-

The Preface.

corruptions, and plainely perceiue, what things there were in my nature, that God had a quarrell against: and so might bee guided by the very finger of God to know the faults, I should set my selfe most against in mortification.

Thirdly, in reading one shall finde sometimes certaine rules or counsells giuen, which one sensibly is affected withall, and hath an inward desire, Oh that I could but remember this counsell of the holy Ghost. Now I would note all those places, that the holy Ghost made me in loue withall in the reading, that might concerne my own particular direction either at home, or abroad.

Againe,

The Preface.

Againe, the most people in the midst of these extreame differences of [...] *feele somet*[...] *desire, suc*[...] *could tell b*[...] *what to be*[...] *the world* [...] *Now for* [...] *all those* [...] *containe* [...] *truth, against which there can be in my conscience no cauill, but I could liue and die in the assurance, that that is the wil of God. It is incredible, how the simplest may settle themselues herein, in all the fundamentall points of religion. If thou finde of these but* 20.30.40. *or* 50. *places in the whole Bible; thou*

canst

Handwritten note: Nicholas Byfield, Directions for the private reading of the Scriptures

The Preface.

canst not now beleeue, how it will settle thee : As for example, 1 Ioh. 5. he saith, There are three in heauen, the Father, the Word, and the Spirit, and these three are one. All the world now should neuer make me doubt of the Trinitie in vnitie. When I had gotten those grounds, those I would sticke to, and for other questions, let them wrangle while they will, I would receiue further light when I saw it cleere, but their quarrelling should not much trouble me. And thus I might go on with the particulars of the first sort of rules, but these shall suffice to giue light to the course.

Now for the second sort of
Rules

The Preface.

Rules one may finde in every place certaine things, strongly obiected against the practise of the godly: As for example, that they deserue to bee hated, because they will not keepe company with their neighbours, and because they stand so precisely vpon small matters, as lesser othes, and doing slight workes vpon the sabbath day, and such like: and besides, many men are afraide to enter vpon such a course of life, because it is a way so euill spoken of, and reproched in the world &c. Now for my owne establishment I would marke, where my course differed from other men, and in reading I would gather euident places, that might warrant my

practise

The Preface.

practise: As for example, places that iustifie the auoiding of the company of the wicked, and so againe places, that shew, that the sincere practise of godlines hath beene euer liable to the scornes, reproches, and slaunders of the world. And so of the rest.

Now for the maner of using these rules, I thinke, thou maist profitably follow these directions. First make thee a little paper booke of a sheete or two of paper, as may be most portable: then write vpon the toppe of euery leafe the title for that that thou wouldest obserue in reading. Chuse out only six or eight titles out of the whole number of such as for the present

The Preface.

sent thou hast most neede to obserue: or onely so many as thou art sure thy memory will easily cary to thy reading, whether more or fewer. In reading obserue onely such places as stare thee in the face, that are so euident, thy heart cannot looke of them. Trouble not thy selfe with that obiection, that there are many things which thou canst not discerne, take thou onely such as thou canst not passe ouer, they are so cleare and euident. In noting the places, set downe vnder each title only the booke, Chapter, and verse, and not the words, for that will tire thee in the end: As for example, would I obserue all the hard places, which

The Preface.

in reading I haue a desire to know the meaning of, that so when I come into the company of Preachers or able Christians, I might haue profitable questions to propound: I would set it downe thus,

Hard places,
    Malach. 4. 5.
    Malach. 2. 6.

And so of other places: for I giue these on the suddaine but for instance sake. Now when thou hast done thy quarters taske, or thy yeeres taske, then thou maist write out the choisest things, as thou thinkest good, and in the meane time hast the vse of the places for turning to. And if thou shouldest in reading, of thy selfe remem-

The Preface.

remember some title, which thou hast not in this direction, and yet hast a great desire to obserue places of that kinde, by any meanes write it downe, whilest thou thinkest of it, and custome in obseruing will make thee able to bee thine owne Directour hereafter. Looke not at the profit of this course the first weeke, or month: but consider, how rich it will make thee at the yeeres end. I am perswaded, if thou feare God, thou wouldst not sell thy collections for a great price, after thou hast gathered them, if it were but for the good, they may doe thee in the euill day, when it shall come vpon thee.

 Farewell, the Lord giue thee

THE

The order of the
Bookes, and of reading the whole SCRIPTVRES.

He *Booke* you are to read is the Bible: *your Bible* is diuided into 2: parts, the old *Testament*, and the *New*.

The olde TESTAMENT containes the Law and the Prophets.

The Law is expressed in the fiue bookes of *Moses*, called the *Pentateuche*.

The PROPHETS, comprehend three kindes of writings:

B   1: Histo-

The order of the bookes and

1. History (principally) from *Iosua* to *Iob*, called the anterior Prophets.
2. Doctrine (principally) from *Iob* to *Esay*, called the *Hagiographa*.
3. Prophesie specially taken (principally) from *Esay* to the end of *Malachy*, called the posterior Prophets.

The new Testament containes:

1. History (principally) in the foure *Euangelists*, and the *Actes*.
2. Doctrine (principally) in the *Epistles*.
3. Prophesie in the *Reuelation*.

That, which you are first then to read, is the *Law* in the fiue bookes of *Moses*:

which bookes intreate,
1. First of the originall and state

state of the Church, in the beginning (to whom the *Law* was giuen) in *Genesis*.

2. Secondly of the promulgation or publication of the *Law*, which was giuen either generally, the lawes *Ecclesiasticall*, and *Politicall* together, and so in *Exod*. 9. or specially and apart, and so the Lawes *Ecclesiasticall* are giuen in *Leuiticus*, the Lawes *Politicall* are giuen in *Numbers*.

3. Thirdly the repetition of the Law in *Deuteronomy*.

4 The order of the bookes and

GENESIS.

IN *Genesis* you shall read:
1. First of the creation of the Church, chap: 1. 2. 3.
2. Secondly of the constitution of the Church. from Chapter 4. to the end.

In the creation obserue the making,

First of the *World*, in which the Church was to liue, Chap. 1.

Secondly of *Man*, of which it was to consist: in whom consider

His *happinesse*, in which hee was made, Chapt: 2.

of reading the Scriptures.

Chapter 2.

His *misery*, into which he fell, chap. 3.

The constitution of the Church must bee considered as it was in the two worlds: the *olde* world before the floode, from chap. 4. to 8. and the *new world* after the floode, of which chapter 8. to the ende of the booke.

In the old world consider.

The propagation of sinne and punishment, chap. 4.

The conseruation of the Church, chap. 5.

The condemnation of that sinfull world:

Foretold, chap. 6.

Executed, chap. 7.

The story of the *new world* is considered chiefly in the ages of foure men: that is *Noah* to ch: 12. *Abraham* to ch: 25. *Isaach*

6 *The order of the bookes and*
to ch: 28. and *Iacob* from ch: 28. to the end of the booke.

In the history of *Noah* consider,

His deliuerance from the Deluge, chap. 8.

His blessing from GOD, chap. 9.

His Familie and Posteritie.

As it was vnited, chap. 10.

As it was dispersed through the earth, Chap. 11. whereof the election of a peculiar people out of the rest to God, of whom the Church consisted.

In the History of *Abraham* consider,

First his vocation chap: 12. first part.

Secondly his peregrination both in *Ægipt* chap. 12. and in
Canaan

Canaan chap. 13.

Thirdly, his dealing,

First with *Lot* chap. 14.

Secondly with God: with God I say, who promised him issue chapt. 15. gaue him issue of *Sarah* chapter 16. and makes his couenant with him, chap: 17. to 25.

About the Couenant obserue,

First the *forme* of it, chap. 17.
Secondly the *fruit* of it.

First on Gods part, which was shewed in the communication.

Of *Counsells* and secrets vnto him Chap. 18.

Of *Benefits* in deliuering *Lot* chap. 19. In succouring the weakenesse

The order of the bookes and

  of *Abraham* chap. 20. and giuing the promised child chap. 21.

 Secondly on *Abrahams* part, who is commended,

  For the obedience of his faith, chap. 22.

  For his humanitie, chap. 23.

  For his piety in disposing of his sonne in marriage, chap. 24.

 Thus of *Abraham*.

The History of *Isaach* containes,

  His kindred and issue, chap. 25.

  His trauailes and troubles, ch: 26.

  His prophesie concerning the estate of the Church in the posterity of his two sonnes, ch: 27.

 Thus of *Isaach*.

The History of *Iacob* is diuided according to his threefold peregrination,

1. Into *Mesopotamia*, where note.

His iourney thither, chap. 28.

His arriuall and mariage, chap. 29.

His riches and children, ch: 30.

2. Into *Canaan*, where note

His iourney, ch: 31.

His arriuall, where note

His *congresse* with *Esau*, chapter 32. 33.

His *progresse* with much griefe and miserie, for there

The rauishing of *Dina*, chap. 34.

The death of Rachell,

The order of the bookes and chell, chap. 35.
The selling of *Ioseph*, chap. 37.
The inceſt of *Iuda*, chap. 38.

3. Into *Egipt*, where conſider
1. The going downe of his children, and ſo went
  1. *Ioseph*, of whoſe afflictions read c: 39. and 40. and dignitie and preferment chap. 41.
  2. The other brethren of whom chap. 42. 43. and 44.
2. The going downe of *Iacob* himſelfe, where conſider,
  1. His ſending for, by *Ioſeph*, chap. 45.
  2. His trauailes thither, ch. 46.
  3. His abode there, where

of reading the Scriptures.

where consider
- 1. His conference with the King of *Egipt*, chap. 47.
- 2. His blessing of *Ioseph*, ch: 48.
- 3. His prophesie concerning the posterity of his sons, c: 49.
- 4. His death and buriall, c: 50.

March.

12 The order of the bookes and

March: Genesis.
  1.   1, 2, 3.
  2.   4, 5, 6, 7.
  3.   8, 9, 10, 11.
  4.   12, 13, 14.
  5.   15, 16, 17.
  6.   18, 19, 20, 21.
  7.   22, 23, 24.
  8.   25, 26, 27.
  9.   28, 29, 30.
  10.   31, 32, 33.
  11.   34. 35, 36, 37, 38.
  12.   39, 40, 41.
  13.   42, 43, 44, 45.
  14.   46, 47, 48, 49, 50.
                      Exodus.

of reading the Scriptures. 13

EXODVS.

The booke of *Exodus* intreates of the giuing of the law in generall, and so the story intreates of two things;

First of the deliuerance of the people of *Israell*, to whom God was to publish his law, from ch: 1. to ch: 19. Secondly of the Lawes themselues, chap: 19. to the end of the booke.

In the story of the deliuerance of the *Israelites* consider,

1. The occasion of it.
2. The instrument, by whom it was effected.
3. The deliuerance it selfe.

4. The

4: The consequents of the deliuerance.

The occasion was the tyranny of the *Ægiptians*, ch: 1.

The instrument was *Moses*, concerning whom the story tels
1: Of his birth, chap. 2.
2: Of his calling, chap. 3.
3: Of his assistant *Aaron*, ch: 4.
4: Of the speeches he made to the King of *Egipt*, ch 5. & 6.
5: Of the signes and wonders wrought in *Egipt*, these signes were either

 Confirming signes, ch: 7.
 Or punishment signes, euen ten great plagues vpon the *Egiptians*, chap. 8. 9. 10. 11.

The deliuerance it selfe, wherin consider,
1: Their departure out of *Ægipt*, ch. 12.
2: The ratification of it by signes

of reading the Scriptures. 15

signes & obseruations, c: 13.

: Their passage through the red sea, chap. 14.

. Their thankesgiuing, ch: 15.

The consequents of the delierance were,

: Prouision of victaile and necessaries, ch: 16.

: Defence from enemies, c. 17.

: Administration of iustice, chap: 18.

Thus of the deliuerance of the people: the lawes follow: The Law must bee considered two waies:

First as it was giuen by God, chap: 19. to 31.

Secondly as it was obeyed by the people, ch: 32. to the end.

In the giuing of the Law consider.

: The preparation, ch: 19.

: The diuision; For God gaue them:

1: Morall

1. Morall Lawes, chap. 2
2. Iudiciall Lawes, chap. 21 23.
3. Ceremoniall lawes, chapters, 25. 26. 27. 28. 29. 30. 31.

The obedience of the people must be considered either in respect.

1. Of the morall Law, where note

    Their transgression, ch: 32.

    Their reconciliation with God, ch: 33.

    The restitution of the Law, ch: 34.

2. Of the Ceremoniall Lawe wherein is set downe the story of the building of the Tabernacle, ch: 35. to the end of the booke.

March.

of reading the Scriptures. 17

March: Exodus.

15.   1, 2, 3.

16.   4, 5, 6.

17.   7, 8, 9, 10, 11.

18.   12, 13, 14.

19.   15, 16, 17.

20.   18, 19, 20.

21.   21, 22, 23.

22.   24, 25, 26, 27.

23.   28, 29, 30, 31.

24.   32, 33, 34.

25.   35. to the end of the booke.

LEVI-

LEVITICVS.

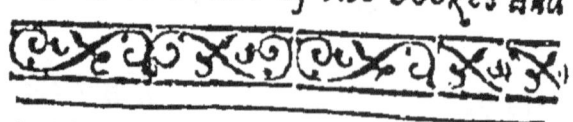

THe booke called *Leuiticu* intreates,

   First of Sacrifices.

   Secondly of sacred Persons.

The Sacrifices must be considered, either in respect,

   First of their *sorts* : chapters 1. 2. 3. 4. 5.

   Secondly of the *rites* about them, chap: 6. 7.

The *sorts* of Sacrifices must be considered, as they were distinguished either

   First by the matter, of which they were, and so they were either,

     Of liuing creatures chap. 1.

     Of things without life, chap. 2.

Second-

of reading the Scriptures. 19

Secondly by the occasions, for which they were, and these were either,

Good things receiued from God, chap. 3. or

Euill things done by man, chap. 4. 5.

Thus of Sacrifices.

The Persons are either,

Publike, of whom, c: 8. to 11.

Private, ch: 11. to the end.

The publike persons were the Priests, concerning whom obserue,

First their consecration to their offices, ch: 8.

Their execution of their offices, ch: 9.

Thirdly their transgression in their offices, ch: 10.

The priuate Persons are considered in respect of their sanctification, and this sanctification was either,

Particu-

20 *The order of the bookes and*

    Particular: of one man, c
11. to 16. or

    Commune of the who
Church, ch: 16. to the end.

  The sanctification of one m
in particular is considered of,
respect of the waies by which
was polluted, as

1. By eating, ch. 11.
2. By childbearing, ch. 12.
3. By leprosie, ch: 13. 14.
4. By Fluxe, ch. 15.

  The common sanctificatio
of the whole Church is to be
considered,

    First in things necessary, cl
16. to 27.

    2. In things voluntary, c: v
  About things necessary, co
sider,

1. The Lawes, ch: 16. to 26.
2. The oblignation of them
promises & threatnings,
  The Lawes concerne eithe
                Pu

of reading the Scriptures.

Purification for their sinnes, chap. 16. 17. Or

Information of their liues, chap. 18. to 26.

The purification was either,
Ordinary and annuall, c: 16.
Or Extraordinary, ch. 17.

The lawes that concerned the information of their liues were either,

Oeconomicall about their mariages, ch: 18. Or

Politicall, about their cariage abroad with others, chapters 19. 20. Or

Ecclesiasticall, which Lawes considered either,
Persons, ch. 21. Or
Things, ch. 22. Or
Times, viz.
{ Dayes, chap. 23. 24.
Yeares, cha: 25.

March

March:	Leuiticus.
26:	1:2:3:4:5.
27:	6:7:8:9:10.
28:	11:12:13:14:15.
29:	16:17:18:19.
30:	20:21:22:23.
31:	24:25:26:27.

NVMBERS.

THe booke of *Numbers* intreates of Lawes, and those lawes *politicall* for the most part, that were occasioned by the mustering of the people for their iourney to *Canaan*.

The History concernes,

1. Their *preparation* to the iourney, ch: 1. to ch: 11.

2. Their *iournies*, ch: 11. to 22.

3. Their *station* or abode, when they came neere to *Canaan*, chapt. 22. to the ende of the booke.

In their preparation to the iourney obserue,

1 Their mustering or numbring.

2: The Lawes giuen them.
3: The manner.
 The muster was either *ciuil* of the *people*, who are
   Numbred, ch: 1.
   Ordred, chap: 2.
 Or *sacred* of the *Priests*, who are,
   Numbred, ch: 3.
   Ordred, chap: 4.
 The Lawes are either *common* to all, about sanctity, in things
  Necessary, ch: 5.
  Voluntary, ch: 6.
 Or particular.
 First *ciuill* for the Tribes, chap: 7.
 Secondly *sacred* for the *priests* and *Leuites*, ch: 8.
 Their manner is double,
1. Of their sanctification, and order, ch: 9.
2. Of their iournies, ch: 10.
 Thus of their preparation.
      Their

Their iournies are distinguished by a story of eight murmurings of the people.

The first was for the tediousnesse of their iourney.

The second was for wearines of the *Manna*, ch: 11.

The third was the emulation of *Miriam*, and *Aaron* against *Moses*, chap. 12

The fourth was the sedition of the spies ⎰ murmuring, ch. 13.
⎱ plagued, ch. 14.
⎰ reconciled, ch. 15.

The fift was the conspiracie of the three *Leuites*, ch: 16.

The sixt was the indignation of the people at the former iudgements, where note

Their murmuring, c. 17.

Their reconciliation as it respects

The order of the bookes and

    Persons and rites, ch. 18.

    The manner, ch. 19.

The seuenth was for want of water, chap. 20.

The eight was for the tediousnes of the way, ch. 21.

    Thus of their iournies.

Their *station* or abode hath a double story,

    One concernes the people that were to inherit.

    The other concernes the inheritance it selfe.

The people are considered, as they were,

    Conquerours of their enemies, ch. 22.

    Encountred by *magicke arts*, ch. 22. 23. 24.

    Disordred with idolatry and fornication, ch. 25.

    Reconciled and a new mustered, ch. 26.

        Furnished

of reading the Scriptures. 27

Furnished with a new *Prince*, chap: 27.

Instructed about sacred things.

    Necessary, ch. 28. 29.

    Voluntary, chap. 30.

The inheritance is considered,

First in a part of it which was

    Conquered, ch. 31.

    Disposed, ch. 32.

    By a digression their iournies are reckoned altogether, ch. 33.

Secondly in the whole, where consider,

    The boundes and diuision of the land, ch. 34.

    The lawes concerning the inheritance, either as it was

        Sacred, chap. 35.

        Ciuill, for the people, chap. 36.

The order of the bookes and

Aprill: *Numbers.*

1.   1, 2, 3, 4.
2.   5, 6, 7, 8.
3.   9, 10, 11.
4.   12, 13, 14, 15.
5.   16, 17, 18, 19.
6.   20, 21, 22.
7.   23, 24, 25, 26.
8.   27, 28, 29, 30.
9.   31, 32, 33.
10.   34, 35, 36.

Deutero-

Deuteronomie.

THe booke of *Deuteronomie* containes the repetition of the Law, wherein consider,

First, how the people are prepared to receiue the Law, c. 1. to ch. 5.

2. How the Law is giuen, ch: 5. to ch. 27.

3. How the Law is confirmed, ch. 27. to the end.

The people are prepared.

1. By rehearsall of Gods blessings in *peace*, ch. 1.

2. By good successe in warre, chapters, 2. 3.

3. By counsell, ch: 4.

In the giuing of the law consider,

The order of the bookes and

1. The propounding of it, c. 5.
2. The expounding of it, this exposition concernes,
   1. The morall law:
      more generally, c: 6. 7. 8. 9. 10. 11.
      more specially, c. 12. 13
   2. The ceremoniall law, ch. 14. 15. 16.
   3. The iudiciall law, the iudiciall law I say, as it was either

      Common to all. c. 17.
      Singular, and so concerned

         The Priest, c. 18.
         The people, c. 19.
         The warre, chap. 20.
         The courts of ciuill Iustice, c. 21. to 27.

The law is confirmed,
1. By signes, ch. 27.

2. By

of reading the Scriptures.

2. By promises and threatnings, chap. 28.
3. By the renuing of the couenant, ch. 29. 30.
4. By the election of a new Captaine, ch. 31.
5. By prophecies, ch: 32. 33.

All conclude with the history of *Moses* death, ch. 34.

Aprill:	*Deuteronomie.*
11.	1. 2. 3. 4.
12.	5. 6. 7.
13.	8. 9. 10.
14.	11. 12. 13.
15.	14. 15. 16.
16.	17. 18. 19. 20.
17.	21. 22. 23.
18.	24. 25. 26.
19.	27. 28.
20.	29. 30. 31.
21.	32. 33. 34.

Hitherto of the Law, the Prophets follow.

The Prophets, that were hiſtoricall, intreat of the Church of the Iewes, either

   Of their comming into Canaan, ſo *Ioſhua.*

Or of their condition after they had that Land for their inheritance, and that

1. Till the captiuity:
   1. Vnder Iudges, the bookes of *Iudges* and *Ruth.*
   2. Vnder Kings, and ſo the bookes of *Samuel*, *Kings*, and *Chronicles*,
2. After the captiuitie; of things done,
   1. In *Iudea*, and ſo the bookes of *Eſdras* and *Nehemiah*:
   2. In *Babilon*, and ſo *Heſter.*

Ioſhua.

of reading the Scriptures. 33

IOSHVA.

Concerning *Ioshua* three things may be obserued,
1. His calling to the gouernement, ch: 1.
2. His Actes.
   1. In time of warre: where note
      1. The sending of the spies, chap. 2.
      2. Their passing ouer *Iordan* miraculously with the consequents of it, c: 3. 4. 5.
      3. The besieging and winning of *Hierico*, ch. 6. 7.
      4. The winning of *Hai*, c. 8.
      5. The couenant with the

C 5 Gibeon-

34 *The order of the bookes and Gibeonites ignorantly made,* chap. 9.
   6. The victory ouer 5. kings, chap. 10.
   7. Battaile with the remnant of the *Canaanites*, ch: 11.
   8. All repeated, ch: 12.
2. In the time of peace:
   1. The diuision of the Land, chap. 13. to 21.
   2. The dimission of the trans-Iordanians, ch. 22.
   3. The celebration of a Parliament, chap. 23.
3. His death, chap: 24.

Aprill.   *Ioshua.*

22.	1. 2. 3. 4. 5.
23.	6. 7. 8. 9. 10. 11.
24.	12. 13. 14. 15. 16.
25.	17. 18. 19. 20. 21.
26.	22. 23. 24.

Iudges.

of reading the Scriptures. 35

IVDGES.

The booke of *Iudges* containes the History of the Iewes vnder the gouernment of Iudges, where note

1. The occasion of this gouernment, ch: 1. 2.
2. The narration of the peoples estate,
    1. Vnder Gouernours;
        1. Of *Hothniel*, and *Ehud*, and *Sangar*, ch: 3.
        2. Of *Deborah*, ch: 4. 5.
        3. Of *Gedeon*, ch: 6. 7. 8.
        4. Of *Abimelech*, ch: 9.
        5. Of *Iephtha*, c: 10. 11. 12.
        6. Of *Sampson*, chapters 13. to 17.
    2. With

36 The order of the bookes and

2. Without Gouernours, whereof their monstrous sinnes, and ciuill warre, ch. 17. to the end.

Aprill: Iudges.

27.   1. 2. 3. 4. 5.

28.   6. 7. 8. 9. 10. 11. 12.

29.   13. 14. 15. 16.

30.   17. 18. 19. 20. 21.

RVTH.

of reading the Scriptures. 37

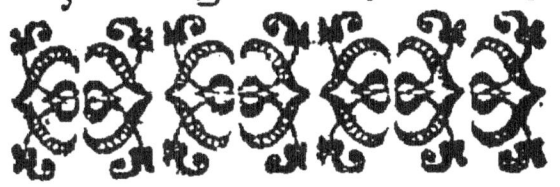

RVTH.

THe booke of *Ruth* entreates of *Ruth* a *moabitish* woman; and so

1. Of her piety: wherein of
    1. Her conuersion, ch. 1.
    2. Of her conuersation, ch. 2.
2. Of her mariage, as it was
    1. Procured, ch. 3.
    2. Celebrated, ch. 4.

May: Ruth.

1.   1. 2. 3. 4.

Hitherto of the history of the Iewes vnder Iudges, their estate vnder Kings till their captiuity followes, and that

1. First

1. First, as the kingdome was vnited, where the kings were first,
   1. By election, of those, 1 *Samuel*.
   2. By succession of these, 2 *Samuel*.
2. Secondly as the kingdome was diuided,
   1. Vnder *Salomon*, 1 *Kings*.
   2. Vnder other Kings, 2: *Kings*.
3. As it was in both estates more fully vnfolded in the 1: and 2: of *Chronicles*.

of reading the Scriptures. 39

1: SAMVEL.

THe first booke of *Samuel* intreates of the estate of the Iewes vnder their Kings Elect: where note,

1. The time of the change of gouernment, *viz.* in the daies of *Samuel*, whose birth is described, ch: 1. and part of the second.

2. The occasion of the change, *viz.* the wickednes, both

    Of *Helies* sonnes, which is

      Discouered, & threatned, ch: 2. 3.

      Punished, c: 4. 5. 6 7.

    And of *Samuels* sons, c: 8.

3. The

3. The story of the Kings, *viz.*

  1. Of *Saul*, of whose, both

    Election, as he was

      Called, ch: 9.

      Confirmed by

        Inauguration, c. 10.

        Consent of the people, ch. 11.

        Resignation of *Samuel*, ch. 12.

        And reiection with the causes of it, ch. 13. 14. 15.

  2. Of *David*.

The history of *David* contains things, that befell him

  First in his prosperous estate, as

    Vocation to the kingdome, chap. 16.

    Victory ouer *Goliah*, c: 17.

  Secondly in his aduersity, & these concerne,

    1. His exile and banishment, where note

        1. The

of reading the Scriptures.

The cause, ch. 18.
The sorts of his exile,
In his owne countrey, chap. 19. 20.
Without the Country.
Amongst the *Philistims*, ch. 21.
Amongst the *Moabites*, ch. 22.

2. His persecutions considered.
1. In the grieuousnesse of them, which appeares
By the diuersitie of the places, whither he fled, c: 23. 24. 35. 26.
By his flight to the enemies, with whom he was faine to liue, where what hee did, ch. 27. 28. 29. 30.
2. In the end of them, chap. 31.

May,

In politicall things, ch. 9.10.

2. Secondly euill, where note

His sinnes committed chap. 11.

Confessed, chap. 12.

His punishmentes, which were either

1. Internall, & domesticall, as

1. The incest of *Ammon*, c: 13.

2. The sedition of *Absalon*, wherein note

The occasion, chap. 14.

The beginning of it, ch: 15.

The progression of it, ch. 16.

The issue of it, ch: 17. 18. 19.

2. Exter-

of reading the Scriptures. 45

2. Externall and publike; these must be considered,
 1. In the sorts of them, *viz.*
  The sedition of *Ziba*, ch. 20.
  The famine, c. 21.
 2. In the euents of them,
  1. Good, *viz.*
   Thankesgiuing, chap. 22.
   Prophesie, c: 23.
  2. Euill, ch. 24.

---

ay: 2. *Samuel.*

1. 2. 3. 4.
5. 6. 7. 8. 9. 10.
11. 12. 13.
14. 15. 16. 17. 18. 19.
20. 21. 22. 23. 24.

1. *Kings*

1: KINGS.

THe first booke of *Kings* intreates concerning the kingdome,
1. In the increase vnder *Salomon*, where
    1. The instituting of *Salomon* to be King, ch: 1.
    2. The conseruation of him in the kingdome, ch. 2. 3.
    3. The administration of the kingdome, wherein his glory is shewed,
        1. In his family, and subiects, ch: 4.
        2. In his buildings both of the Temple, and his owne house, c: 5. 6. 7. 8. 9
            3. In

of reading the Scriptures.

3. In his riches, chap. 10.
4. In the decrease, concerning which consider
  1. The occasions, or causes of it, *viz.* The sinnes of *Salomon*, and the iustice of God.
  2. The beginnings of it, where consider
    1. The Authours of the diuision. *Rhehoboam* and *Ieroboam*, of whom ch: 12. 13. 14.
    2. Their successors whose raignes are handled
      More briefly, c: 15.
      More largely in the raigne of *Ahab* from ch: 16. to the end.

48 *The order of the bookes and*

May: 1: Kings.

14:             1: 2: 3: 4.

15:             5: 6: 7: 8: 9:

16:             10: 11: 12: 13: 14.

17:             15. 16: 17: 18:

18:             19: 20: 21: 22.

2. Kings.

2. Kings.

THe second booke of *Kings* containes a history of the decrease of the kingdomes of *Israel* and *Iuda*, and they are considered,

First in their continuance and defection together, and so the story entreates of them two waies:

First *apart* where the succession and actes of the Kings of *Israel* are noted, as of

Ahasiah, ch. 1.
Ioram, from ch. 2. to 9.
Iehu, ch. 9. 10.
Ioash, ch. 11. 12.
Iehoas and *Ioas* together, 13.

2. Secondly together both the kingdomes are considered in their story from ch: 14. to 18.
2. Secondly in a speciall storie about the destruction of the Iewish kingdome, where consider,
   1. Their decay, ch. 18. 19. 20. 21.
   2. Their repaire, ch. 22. 23.
   3. Their finall destruction, chap. 24. to the end.

May.	2. Kings.
19.	1. 2. 3. 4. 5.
20.	6. 7. 8. 9. 10.
21.	11. 12. 13. 14. 15. 16.
22.	17. 18. 19. 20. 21.
23.	22. 23. 24. 25.

Iudges.

of reading the Scriptures.

1: *Chronicles.*

THe first booke of the *Chronicles* intreates,

First of the beginning of the kingdome of *Israell*, where obserue the Genealogie,

  1. Generall of the world and all nations from *Adam* to *Iacob*, chap. 1.

  2. Particular of the nation of the *Israelites* in their 12. Tribes, ch. 2. to 9.

2. Of the administration of the kingdome,

  1. Vnder *Saul*, ch: 9. 10.

  2. Vnder *Dauid*, in whom consider,

    1. His entrance into his king-

The order of the bookes and kingdome, where note,

 His inauguration, chap. 11.

 His followers, chapters, 11. 12.

 His care of religion, chap. 13.

 His confirmation in the kingdome, ch. 14.

2. His acts,

 1. In the progresse of his raigne both

  1. Good; and these
   For religion and Gods seruice, chap. 15. 16. 17.
   For the warre, chap. 18. 19. 20.

  2. Euill, ch: 21.

 Secondly towards the end of his raigne in his old age, where note

  First his courses againe for religion, chap. 22.

of reading the Scriptures.

chap. 22. 23. 24. 25. 26.

Secondly, his order for the Commonwealth, chap. 27.

Thirdly, the parliament a litle before his death, with the euent of it, chap. 28. 29.

May.	1. Chronicles.
24:	1: 2: 3: 4: 5: 6.
25:	7: 8: 9: 10.
26:	11: 12: 13: 14.
27:	15: 16: 17.
28:	18: 19: 20: 21:
29.	22: 23: 24: 25: 26.
30.	27: 28: 29.

2 *Chroni-*

2. Chronicles.

THe second booke of *Chronicles* intreates of the kingdome of *Israel*,

  First in the increase vnder *Salomon*, of whom consider

    His vertues, ch: 1.

    His buildings both sacred ch. 2. to 8. and ciuill, ch. 8.

    His condition and death, ch. 9.

2. Secondly in the decrease in the raignes of

  Rhehoboam, chap. 10. 11. 12.
  Abiah,   chap. 13.
  Asia,   ch. 14. 15. 16.
  Iehosophat, ch. 17. 18. 19. 20.
  Ioram,   ch. 21.
                Abasia,

of reading the Scriptures.

Ahasia,	ch. 22.
Ioash,	ch. 23. 24.
Amasia,	ch. 25.
Vzziah,	ch. 26.
Iotham,	ch. 27.
Ahaz,	ch. 28.
Hezechiah,	ch. 22. 30. 31. 32.
Manasses,	ch. 33.
Ammon,	ch. 33.
Iosiah,	ch. 34. 35.
Iehohaas,	}
Iehoiacim,	} Chap. 36.
Iechoniah,	}
Zedechiah,	}

56 The order of the bookes and

Iune:	2. Chronicles.
1.	1, 2, 3, 4.
2.	5, 6, 7.
3.	8, 9, 10, 11, 12.
4.	13, 14, 15, 16.
5.	17, 18, 19, 20.
6.	21, 22, 23, 24.
7.	25, 26, 27, 28.
8.	29, 30, 31, 32.
9.	33, 34, 35, 36.

EZRA.

Ezra.

THe booke of *Ezra* intreats of the returne of the people from *Babilon*, where
1. Of the manner of it, ch. 1. 2.
2. Of the end: *viz.* the restoring of religion and gouernment, chap. 3.
3. The hinderances,
   1. *Raised*: both by
      Samaritans, chap. 4.
      And the Gouernour of the land of *Canaan*, c. 5.
   2. *Remooued*,
      By *Cyrus*, chap. 6.
      By *Ezra*, of whose iourny, chap. 7. 8.
      And reformation, which he wrought, chap. 9. 10.

58 The order of the bookes and

Iune: Ezra;

10.   1, 2, 3.
11.   4, 5, 6.
12.   7, 8, 9, 10.

Nehemiah.

13.   1, 2, 3, 4.
14.   5, 6, 7.
15.   8, 9, 10.
16.   11, 12, 13, 14.

Hester.

17.   1, 2, 3.
18.   4, 5, 6.
19.   7, 8, 9, 10.

NEHE-

Nehemiah.

The booke of *Nehemiah* intreates,
First of the repaire of the buildings, and so
    Of the causes of it, ch: 1.2.
    Of the worke it selfe, as
      Begunne, ch. 3.
      Hindered, ch. 4. 5. 6.
      Finished, ch. 6.
2. Of reformation, both
    Politicall, and
    Ecclesiasticall, ch. 7. 8. 9.
10. 11. 12. 13. 14.

ESTER.

ESTER.

THe booke of *Ester* containes a story of the deliuerance of the *Iewes*, and that miraculously, where you may note

1. The meanes of it, *viz. Hester* chap. 1. 2.
2. The manner of it, where note
    1. The greatnesse of the danger, ch. 3.
    2. The degrees of deliuerance:
        1. The intercession of the Queene, chap. 4. 5.
        2. The frustrating of the deuise

of reading the Scriptures. 61

deuise of *Haman*, chap. 6. 7.

3. The consummation of it, where

The reuocation of the decree, chap. 8.

The punishing of aduersaries, ch. 9.

The tranquillitie of the Iewes, ch. 10.

Hitherto of the historicall Prophets. The dogmaticall Prophets, or such as wrote Narations of doctrine chiefly, folow, and these wrote

Either of a singular and particular subiect, as *Iob*: Or

Of a common subiect belonging to all, and so did both

Dauid in meeter, the *Psalmes*.

And *Salomon*,

In Prose, *Prou. Eccles.*
In Verse, *Canticles.*

Iob

IOB.

THe booke of *Iob* containes,
First, a Dialogue in which note,
    1. The occasion, *viz.*
        His prosperitie, ch. 1.
        His aduersitie, ch. 2.
        His sinne, chap. 3.
    2 The sorts, and so obserue the speeches,
        1. Of the Disputants,

    1. { *Eliphas*, ch. 4. 5.
       { *Iob*, ch. 6. 7.
    2. { *Bildad*, ch. 8.
       { *Iob*, ch. 9. 10.
    3. { *Zophar*, ch. 11.
       { *Iob*, ch. 12. 13. 14.
        4. *Eliphas*

of reading the Scriptures. 63

4. { *Eliphas,* ch. 15.
   Iob, ch. 16. 17.

5. { *Bildad,* ch. 18.
   Iob, ch. 19.

6. { *Zophar,* ch. 20.
   Iob, ch. 21.

7. { *Eliphas,* ch. 22.
   Iob. ch. 23. 24.

8. { *Bildad,* ch. 25.
   Iob. ch. 26. 27. 28.
      29. 30. 31.

2. Of the moderators,
  1. *Elihu,* ch. 32. 33.
  2. *God,* 34. 35. 36. 37.
and so to 41.

2. Secondly an Epilogue, wherin obserue the confession and restitution of *Iob,* ch: 42.

Iune

64 The order of the bookes and

Iune:	Iob.
20.	1, 2, 3.
21.	4, 5, 6, 7.
22.	8, 9, 10.
23.	11. 12. 13, 14.
24.	15, 16, 17, 18.
25.	19, 20, 21.
26.	22. 23. 24.
27.	25, 26, 27, 28.
28.	29, 30, 31.
29.	32, 33, 34, 35, 36, 37.
30.	38, 39, 40, 41, 42.

Prouerbes.

of reading the Scriptures. 65

Prouerbes.

THe booke of *Prouerbes* intreates of rules of life,
1. Generall about piety, wherein note
    1. What we must doe, ch. 1. 2. 3. 4. 8. 9.
    2. What we must auoide, ch. 5. 7.
2. Speciall, and so the life of man is formed by all sorts of rules:
    Politicall.
    Oeconomicall.
    Morall, from ch. 10. to the end of the *booke*.
                                Iuly.

The order of the bookes and

Iuly.   Prouerbes.

1.   1. 2. 3. 4.
2.   5. 6. 7.
3.   8. 9. 10.
4.   11. 12. 13.
5.   14. 15. 16.
6.   17 18. 19.
7   20. 21. 22.
8.   23. 24. 25.
9   26. 27. 28.
10.   29. 30. 31.

Ecclesi-

of reading the Scriptures. 67

Ecclesiastes.

THe booke of *Ecclesiastes* intreates,

Of the vanitie of all earthly things prooued by *Salomons* obseruations,

1. In his owne estate, ch: 1.2.
2. In the conditions of all sorts of other men, ch. 3. to ch. 10.

Of rules to bee obserued in this vaine life of ours, ch. 10. 11. 12.

y: *Ecclesiastes.*
    1. 2. 3.
    4. 5. 6.
    7. 8. 9.
    10. 11. 12.
              Canticles.

Canticles.

THe *Canticles* containe excellent descriptions of the loue betwixt Christ, and the Church, set downe Dialoguewise in seuerall speeches:

Of *Christ* and the *Church*, c.1.
Of the *Church* & *Christ*, c.2.
Of the *Church*, ch. 3.
Of *Christ*, ch. 4.
Of the *Church*, ch. 5.
Of the *Church* & *Christ*, c.6.
Of the *Church*, ch. 7. 8.

Iuly.	Canticles.
15.	1, 2, 3.
16.	4, 5, 6.
17.	7. 8.

Esay.

ESAY.

The booke of *Esay* contains Prophesies,

Legall, and these
1. Reproue and correct the sinnes of the Iewes, ch. 1. to the 11. with comfort to the Elect, ch. 11. 12.

Threaten,
1. The enemies of Gods people, wherenote
   The Nations particularly threatned, from ch. 13. to ch. 24.
   The generall vses of these threatnings, ch. 24. 25. 26. 27.
2. The *Israelites*, ch. 28.
3. The *Iewes* themselus, whose captiuitie is denounced with mixture of comforts

The order of the bookes and for the godly in the things of a better world in *Christ* ch. 29. to ch. 36.

Or thirdly are historicall, ch. 36. 37. 38. 39.

2. Are Euangelicall,
  1. Concerning deliuerance from and preseruation in the captiuitie, ch: 40. to 49.
  2. Concerning the kingdom of Christ, about which there are eight Sermons or speeches,
    1. Of Christ, c. 49 50. 51.
    2. Of God, ch. 52.
    3. Of the Prophets expounding
    1. The story of Christ, ch. 53.
    2. The fruite of the kingdome of Christ, c. 54.
    4. Of God promising, c. 55. Exhorting, ch: 56. 57

of reading the Scriptures.

5. Of the Prophet reproving hypocrisie, c. 58 59. Exciting the Church, chap. 60.
6. Of Christ, ch. 61. 62.
7. Of the Church, ch. 63. 64. 65.
8. Of God, chap. 66.

      Esay.

1. 2. 3. 4.
5. 6. 7. 8.
9. 10. 11. 12.
13. 14. 15. 16.
17. 18. 19. 20.
21. 22. 23. 24.
25. 26. 27.
28. 29. 30. 31.
32. 33. 34.
35. 36. 37. 38. 39.
40. 41. 42.

29.

29.   43, 44, 45.

30.   46, 47, 48.

31.   49, 50, 51.

Auguſt.   Eſay.

1.   52. 53. 54.

2.   55, 56, 57.

3.   48, 59, 60.

4.   61, 62, 63.

5.   64, 65, 66.

IEREMY.

IEREMY.

The booke of *Ieremy* hath three things,
1. A Prologue concerning the calling of the Prophet, ch. 1.
2. Sermons that concerne,
   1. The Iewes: either in *Iudea* in the raigne of
      Iosiah, ch. 2. to ch. 21.
      Zedechiah, ch. 21. to 25.
      Iehoiachim, c. 25. 26. 27
      Zedechiah againe, ch. 28. to 35.
      Iehoiachim againe, ch. 31. to 36.
      Of *Zedechia* againe, c. 37. to 43.
      Or in *Egipt*, chap. 34. to 46.
   2. The enemies of the *Iewes*,

74 *The order of the bookes and*
from, ch. 46. to ch. 52.
3. An Epilogue historical, c. 52.

August.   *Ieremie.*

6.   1. 2. 3.
7.   4. 5. 6.
8.   7. 8. 9.
9.   10. 11. 12.
10.   13. 14. 15.
11.   16. 17. 18.
12.   19. 20. 21.
13.   22. 23. 24.
14.   25. 26. 27.
15.   28. 29. 30.
16.   31. 32. 33.
17.   34. 35. 36.
18.   37. 38. 39.
19.   40. 41. 42.
20.   43. 44. 45.
21.   46. 47. 48.
22.   49. 50. 51. 52.

Lamentations.

of reading the Scriptures. 75

Lamentations.

THe *Lamentations* containe the mournings,
Of the Church, ch. 1.
Of the Prophets, ch. 2.
Of the Church, ch. 3.
Of the Prophet, ch. 4.
Of the Church, ch. 5.

August.   Lamentations.

3.   1. 2.
4.   3. 4. 5.

E 2   *Ezekiel,*

Ezechiell.

THe booke of *Ezechiell*, containes
1. The Preface, which concerneth,
    1. God and his maiesty, c. 1.
    2. The Prophet, and his
        Fearefulnesse, ch. 2.
        Confirmation, ch. 3.
2. The prophesies themselues, which containe,
    1. Chiefly *obiurgation* or reproofe of the impiety of the Iewes, with their iudgements in 17. Sermons, from ch. 4. to ch. 25.
    2. *Commination* against the enemies of the Iewes, in 8. Sermons, from ch: 25. to ch. 33.

Exhor-

of reading the Scriptures.

3. *Exhortation* and encouragements to the Iewes, both to repentance, and the hope of deliuerance in 6. Sermons, from ch. 33. to ch. 40.

4. *Consolation* in one continued prophesie of their spirituall deliuerance by Christ: in Visions, c. 40. to the end of the booke.

August.	*Ezechiell.*
25.	1. 2. 3.
26.	4. 5. 6. 7.
27.	8. 9. 10. 11.
28.	12. 13. 14.
29.	15. 16. 17.
30.	18. 19. 20.
31.	21. 22. 23. 24.
September.	
1.	25. 26. 27. 28.
2.	29. 30. 31. 32.

78 *The order of the bookes and*

3.	33. 34. 35.
4.	36. 37. 38.
5.	39. 40. 41.
6.	42. 43. 44.
7.	45. 46. 47. 48.

DANIEL.

The booke of *Daniel* containes,

1. A history of things done both in the *Babylonian* and *Persian* kingdomes, c. 1. to 7.
2. A prophesie of things to be done,
   1. Many calamities to be executed, ch. 7. to 12.
   2. The finall deliuerance and glory of the Elect, ch. 12.

September.	*Daniel.*
8.	1. 2. 3.
9.	4. 5. 6.
10.	7. 8. 9.
11.	10. 11. 12.

Hosea.

HOSEA.

The Prophesie of *Hosea* is either,

Parabolicall, and so the prophesie is,
  1. Propounded, ch. 1.
  2. Applied, ch. 2.
  3. Repeated, ch. 3.

Or plaine, and so it is either,
  A commination & inuectiue in three Sermons:
    The first, chap. 4.
    The second, chap. 5. 6. 7.
    The third, chap. 8. 9. 10.
  Or a consolation, ch. 11. 12. 13. 14.

September,	Hosea.
12.	1. 2. 3.
13.	4. 5. 6. 7.
14.	8. 9. 10.
5.	11. 12. 13. 14.

IOEL.

THe Prophesie of *Ioel* containes
1. A commination of famine, chap. 1.
2. An exhortation to repentance, chap. 2.
3. A consolation to the penitent, chap. 3.

AMOS.

THe Prophesie of *Amos* containes,
1. A commination, both Againſt the enemies of Gods people, chap. 1.

And

of reading the Scriptures. 85

And against the Iewes, and *Israelites*:
1. In plaine words against
    Their idolatry, ch. 2.
    Their violence, ch. 3.
    Their iniquity, pride, inhumanity, and luxurie, chap. 4. 5. 6.
2. In a threefold type, ch. 7. 8. 9.
2. A consolation, from the 11 of ch. 9. to the end.

OBADIAH.

THe Prophet OBADIAH doth
Terrifie, to 12. verse.
Dehort, to verse 17.
Comfort, to the end.

IONAH.

THe Prophesie of *Ionah*, discribes the two callings of *Ionah*;

In the first there is
- The manner, chap. 1.
- The effect, *viz.* his praier, chap. 2.

In the second there is,
- His Sermon to the *Ninevites*, with their repentance, chap. 3.
- The effect of their repentance in *Ionah*, ch. 4.

MICAH.

MICAH.

The Prophesie of *Micah* containes fiue Sermons,

The 1. hath in it threatnings against the whole kingdome, ch. 1. 2.

The 2. hath in it threatnings against the Magistrates, c. 3.

The 3. hath in it a consolation in God, & the *Messiah*, c. 4. 5.

The 4. a commination, ch. 6.

The 5. a consolaton againe, c. 7.

NAHVM

The Prophet *Nahum* threatens destruction to the Assirians, which is

Propounded, chap. 1.

The meanes shewed, ch. 2.
The cause, *viz.* their sinnes, chap. 3.

HABACVK.

THe Prophesie of *Habacuk* containes,
1. A Dialogisme between God and the Prophet, c. 1. 2.
2. A praier, ch. 3.

ZEPHONIAH.

THe Prophesie of *Zephonie* hath three Sermons,
1. A commination, ch. 1.
2. An exhortation, ch. 2.
3. A mixture hauing in it both commination and consolation, chap. 3.

HAGGEI.

The Prophet *Haggei*,
1. Exhorts to the building of the Temple, chap. 1.
2. Comforts them especially with his prophesie of the kingdome of Christ, ch. 2.

ZACHERIAH

The Prophesie of *Zachery* containes,
1. Types and Visions, which are,
  1. *Hortatory*, generall to all the people, ch. 1. 2. speciall to the Priests, ch. 3. 4.
  2. *Monitory*, ch. 5. and 6.
  3. Con-

The order of the bookes and

   3. *Consolatory*, chap. 6.
2. Sermons,
   1. *Doctrinall*, of things present about Gods seruice, chap. 7. 8.
   2. *Propheticall* of things, that concerne Christs
      Incarnation, ch. 9. 10.
      Passion, 11. 12. 13.

MALACHY.

The Prophet *Malachy* First chides:
   For perfidiousnesse in Gods seruice, ch. 1.
   For pollution of mariage and blasphemies, ch. 2.
Secondly, comforts in the promise,
   1. Of Christ, ch. 3.
   2. Of his fore-runner, c. 4.
      September.

ptember.   Ioel.

6.   1. 2. 3.
           Amos.
7.   1. 2. 3.
8.   4. 5. 6.
9.   7. 8. 9.
        Obadiah. Ionah.
10.   1. 2. 3. 4.
           Micah.
21.   1. 2. 3. 4.
22.   5. 6. 7.
           Nahum.
23.   1. 2. 3.
           Habacuc.
24.   1. 2. 3.
           Zephaniah.
25.   1. 2. 3.
              Haggei.

88 *The order of the bookes and*

September.   Haggei.
26.   1. 2.
             Zacharie.
27.   1. 2. 3. 4.
28.   5. 6. 7. 8.
29.   9. 10. 11. 12. 13.
             Malachy.
30.   1. 2. 3. 4.

THE

THE NEW
Testament.

MATHEW.

THe Euangelist St *Mathew* intreates of things, that concerne

1. The person of Christ, as his birth, ch. 1. his education, c. 2.
2. His office, where consider,
   1. The preparation to his office : both
     In his fore-runner *Iohn* Baptist, ch. 3.
     And in himself, who was
      Baptised, ch. 3.
      Tempted, ch. 4.
   2. The

2. The execution of his office,

  1. *Propheticall* in teaching: His doctrine must bee considered,

    1. As briefly propounded in one Sermon, chap. 5. 6. 7.

    2. As more largely expounded and confirmed, and so

      1. He teacheth & confirmes it by miracles of all sorts, from ch. 8. to c 19.

      2. Hee reproues and confuteth the practise, and doctrine of the Pharises, from c. 19. to c. 24.

      3. He prophesieth of the destruction of *Ierusalem*, and the world, ch. 24. 25.

  2. *Sacer-*

of reading the Scriptures. 91

2. *Sacerdotall* or priestly in his passion, and sacrifice for the sinnes of the world, ch. 26 27.

3. *Regall*, in respect of the beginning and the manifestation of it, chap. 28.

Feber.   *Mathew.*

1. 2. 3.
4. 5.
6. 7.
8. 9. 10.
11. 12.
13. 14.
15. 16. 17.
18. 19. 20.
21. 22. 23.
24. 25.
26. 27. 28.

MARKE.

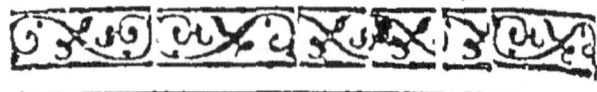

MARKE.

SAINT *Marke* intreates,
1. Of the life of Christ, and therein
    1. Of his fore-runner, ch. 1.
    2. Of things said or done by him,
        1. Before his transfiguration, and so reporteth both his *oracles*, and *miracles* from ch. 2. to c. 9.
        2. In his transfiguration, chap. 9.
        3. After his transfiguration
            1. Before his entrance into the holy City, chap. 10.
            2. In his entrance, where note,
                1. His disputation, chap. 12.

of reading the Scriptures. 93
   chap. 12.
  2. His prediction,
   chap. 13.
Of the passion of Christ, where
1. Of the things, that went before it, ch. 14.
2. Of the manner of it, ch. 15.
3. Of the consequents of it, viz. his buriall, his resurrection, and assention, chap. 16.

---

ober.   *Marke.*

    1: 2.
    3: 4.
    5: 6.
    7: 8.
    9: 10.
    11: 12.
    13: 14.
    15. 16.
     LVKE.

LVKE.

SAINT *Luke* intreates,
1. Of the life of Christ,
    1. Priuate, where of
        His conception, ch. 1.
        His birth and education, chap. 2.
    2. Publike in preaching the Gospell, where
        1. How he was prepared chap. 3.
        2. How he executed it.
            1. Alone,
                By teaching, ch. 4.
                By doing, ch. 5.
            2. With others, *viz.* his disciples, both
                The 12. Apostles whom he calleth and instructeth, ch. 6. 7. 8. and sendeth, ch. 9.

And

of reading the Scriptures. 95

And the 70. disciples, ch. 10.
2. Of his death, where of
  1. The *antecedents* of it.
  2. The manner of it.
  3. The consequents of it.
1. The *antecedents* of his death were the things hee did, and spake.
  1. In his iourny to *Ierusalem*, where he taught:
    1. Of the inward worship of God, where
      First of praier, c. 11.
      2. Of faith, chap. 12.
      3. of repentance, both
        In the causes,
          Moouing to it, chap. 13.
          Hindering of it, chap. 14. and
        In the effects of it, c. 15.
    2. Of the outward worship of God, where note,
      1. What

1. What wee must auoide, viz. the abuse of riches, c. 16. Scandall, chap. 17.
2. What we must do, c. 18.
2. When hee came to *Hierusalem*, where note
How he was receiued, c. 19.
How he disputed, ch. 20.
How he prophesied, ch. 21.
2. The manner of his death, chap. 22. 23.
3. The consequents of his death, ch. 24.

October.	Luke.
20.	1. 2.
11.	3. 4.
22.	5. 6.
23.	7. 8.
24.	9. 10.
25.	11. 12.
26.	13. 14.
27.	15. 16.
28.	17. 18.
29.	19. 20.
30.	21. 22.
31.	23. 24.

IOHN.

IOHN.

SAINT *Iohn* intreates,
1. Of the person of Christ, c. 1.
2. Of the office of Christ, which he performed in his iourny.
  1. To the feast of the passouer.
    1. In *Cana*, from whence he set out, ch. 2.
    2. While hee abode at the feast, ch. 3.
    3. In his returne by *Samaria*, ch. 4.
  2. To the feast of *Pentecost*, where
    He cured the palsie, c. 5.
    He fed the people, c. 6.
  3. To the feast of Tabernacles, where note
    1. His comming to *Hierusalem*, ch. 7.
    2. His abode in *Hierusalem*,

The order of the bookes and lem, where
1. His disputation, c. 8.
2. His workes, chap. 9.
3. His Sermon, ch. 10.
3. His departure from thence, c. 11.
4. To the celebration of the true Passouer: where note about his death,
1. What went before,
1. His deeds, *viz.*
Entrance into the city, chap: 12.
Washing his Disciples feete, ch. 13.
2. His speeches,
1. At supper time, c. 14
2. As they went to the garden:
1. Monitory, ch. 15.
2. Consolatory, c. 16
3. Supplicatory, c. 17
2. The manner of his death and passion, ch: 18. 19.
3. The

of reading the Scriptures. 99

3. The consequents of it, viz. his appearance to his Disciples,
>Conuersing in *Iudea*, chap. 20.
>Fishing in *Galile*, ch. 21.

November.	Iohn.
	1. 2.
	3. 4.
	5. 6.
	7. 8.
	9. 10.
	11. 12.
	13. 14.
	15. 16.
	17. 18.
10.	19. 20. 21.

ACTES.

ACTES.

The Actes of the Apostles containe a history,

First, generall of all the Apostles: where
   1. Of their assembling together, chap. 1.
   2. Of their gifts, ch. 2.
   3. Of their sayings, ch. 3.
2. Especiall,
   1. Of *Peter* with *Iohn*, and others, chap. 4. 5.
   2. Of *Steuen*, ch. 6. 7.
   3. Of *Philip*, ch. 8.
   4. Of *Peter* alone: of whose Miracles, ch. 9.
    Doctrine:

1. Pro-

Propounded, ch. 10.
Defended, ch. 11.
Imprisonment and deliuerance, ch. 12.

5. Of *Paul* and his trauailes,
1. With *Barnabas*, c. 13. 14.
2. With *Silas*, of whose
   1. Departure, where of the first counsell at *Hierusalem*, ch. 15.
   2. Abode in *Asia*, ch. 16. In *Græcia*, ch. 17.
   3. His returne, ch. 18.
3. For the *Ephesians*, where consider,
   1. From whence hee went, ch. 18. v. 23.
   2. By what Places, ch. 19. 20.
   3. Whither he came: First to *Hierusalem*, & what befell him there ch. 21. 22. 23. Secondly to *Cæsarea*,

and what was done,
Vnder *Felix*, ch. 41.
Vnder *Festus*, ch. 25.
Vnder *Agrippa*, 26.
And lastly to *Rome*,
chap. 27. 28.

November.   Actes.

11.   1. 2.
12.   3. 4.
13.   5. 6. 7.
14.   8. 9.
15.   10. 11.
16.   12. 13.
17.   14. 15. 16.
18.   17. 18. 19.
19.   20. 21. 22.
20.   23. 24. 25.
21.   26. 27. 28.

R O.

ROMANS.

IN the Epistle to the *Romans* he intreates,
1. Of iustification, ch. 1.2.3.4.5.
2. Of sanctification, ch. 6 7. 8.
3. Of predestination, c. 9. 10. 11.
4. Of good workes, ch. 12. 13. 14. 15. 16.

1. *Corinthians.*

IN the first Epistle to the *Corinthians*,
1. He reproues,
   For Schismes and factions and hearkning to ambiti-

F 4 ous

ous Teachers, ch: 1.2.3.4.
For inceſt and fornication chap. 5.
For going to Law, ch. 6.
2. He diſputeth,
About mariage, ch. 7.
About things indifferent, ch. 8.9.10.
About the Sacrament of the ſupper, ch. 11.
About the right vſe of ſpirituall gifts, ch. 12.13.14.
About the reſurrection, c.15.
3. He concludes about collections and matters of ſaluation chap. 16.

2. Corinthians.

IN the ſecond Epiſtle to the *Corinthians*,
1. He makes *Apologie* for himſelfe againſt diuers aſperſions ch. 1.2.3.4.5.

2. He

He exhorts,
> To holy life and patience, & of shunning needlesse society with the wicked, ch. 6.
>
> To auoide iudging ill of him, ch. 7.
>
> To mercy and liberalitie, chap. 8.9.
>
> To the sincere respect of him and his *Apostelshippe* & ministery, ch. 10.11.12.

He concludes, ch. 13.

Galathians.

he Epistle to the *Galathians* lee reprooues their backesli-ing, ch. 1.

le intreates of iustification, hap. 2.3.4.

le exhorts to good workes, iap. 5. 6.

Ephesians.

IN the Epistle to the *Ephesians* he intreates,
1. Of matter of faith, ch. 1.2.3.
2. Of workes, chap. 4.5.6.

Philippians.

IN the Epistle to the *Philippians* he makes,
1. A narration of his loue to them, of his afflictions and desire of death, ch. 1.
2. He exhorts,
    To loue and humility, ch. 2.
    To warinesse and progresse both in assurance and sanctitie, ch. 3.
3. He concludes,
    1. with particular exhortation.
    2. With generall commendation, ch. 4.

Coloss.

Colossians.

IN the Epistle to the *Colossians* he intreates of matters,
Of faith, ch. 1. 2.
Of life, chap. 3. 4.

1. Thessalonians.

IN the Epistle to the *Thessalonians* he intreates,
Of their conuersion, ch. 1.
Of the meanes of it, ch. 2.
Of the fruite of it, *viz.* his maruellous loue to them, and care for them, ch. 3.
Of directions for their liues, chap. 4. 5.

2. Thessalonians.

IN the second Epistle to the *Thessalonians*,
He comforts, ch. 1.
He prophesieth, ch. 2.
He exhorts, chap. 4.

1. Timothy.

In the first Epistle to *Timothy*,
He confuteth the erronious Doctors, ch. 1.

He exhorteth about prayer and apparrell, ch. 2.

He enformeth concerning the dutie of Byshops and Deacons, ch. 3.

He prophesieth of the last and euill times, ch. 4.

He ordereth Church Gouernours, ch. 5.

He taxeth seuerall abuses, c. 6.

2. Timothy.

In the second Epistle to *Timothy*,
Hee exhorteth him to perseuerance:

   In the duties of his calling, ch. 1.

   In Christian warfare, c. 2.

of reading the Scriptures. 109

He prophesieth, ch. 3.
Hee chargeth about preaching, and so concludeth, c. 4.

TITVS.

IN the Epistle to *Titus* hee intreates of the duty,
Of Ministers, chap. 1.
Of Hearers, chap. 2. 3.

HEBREWES.

IN the Epistle to the *Hebrewes* he entreates;
1. Of Christ, and so
  1. Of his person.
    His Diuine nature, ch. 1.
    His humane nature, ch. 2.
  2. Of his office, as
    Prophet, ch. 3. 4.
    Priest, ch. 5. to 10.
2. Of the duties of Christians, and so
  Of faith, ch. 11.
  Of holy life, ch. 12. 13.

Iames.

IAMES.

IN the Epistle of *Iames* he intreates,

Of patience, right hearing the word, and true religion, ch. 1.

Of loue and iustification by workes, ch. 2.

Of the tongue, and wisedome, chap. 3.

Of contentions, and presumption, ch. 4.

Of oppression, and swearing, and praier, and admonition, ch. 5.

1. PETER.

THe first Epistle of *Peter* hath in it matter,

Of consolation, ch. 1. to v. 13.

Of exhortation, v. 13. of 1. ch. to v. 8. of ch. 3.

Of dehortation, chap. 3. v. 8. to the end.

And

of reading the Scriptures. 111

And these againe are handled:
  Exhortation, ch. 4. to v. 12.
  Consolation, v. 12. to the end of ch. 4.
  Dehortation impliedly,
  With the conclusion, ch. 5.

2. PETER.

IN the 2. Epistle of *Peter*,
He exhorts to holines, c. 1.
He threatens wicked Teachers, and Apostates, chap. 2.
He prophesieth of the day of iudgement, ch. 3.

1. IOHN.

IN the first Epistle of *Iohn* hee intreates,
Of the benefits of Christ, ch. 1.
Of the office of Christians,
    In loue, ch, 2. 3. 4.
    In faith, ch. 5.

REVE-

REVELATION.

IN the *Revelation* is contained A history of the state of the Churches then, ch. 1.2.3.
  A prophesie.
    Of the world, c. 4.5.6.7.8.9.
      Of the Church.
        In her battailes, ch. 10. to 17.
        In her victories, ch. 17. 18. 19. 20.
        In her eternall glory, chap. 21. 22.

November.	*Romans.*
22.	1.2.
23.	3.4.
24.	5.6.
25.	7.8.
26.	9.10.
27.	11.12.13.

of reading the Scriptures.

8.	14. 15. 16.
	1. *Corinthians.*
19.	1. 2. 3.
30.	4. 5. 6.
Decemb: 1.	7. 8.
2.	9. 10.
3.	11. 12.
4.	13. 14.
5.	15. 16.
	2. *Corinthians.*
6.	1. 2.
7.	3. 4.
8.	5. 6.
9.	7. 8. 9.
10.	10. 11.
11.	12. 13.
	Galathians.
12.	1. 2.
13.	3. 4.
14.	5. 6.
	Ephesians.
15.	1. 2.
16.	3. 4.
17.	5. 6.
	Philippians.

114 The order of the bookes and

    Philippians.
18.   1. 2.
19.   3. 4.
    Colossians.
20.   1. 2.
21.   3. 4.
    1. Thessalonians.
22.   1. 2. 3.
23.   4. 5.
    2. Thessalonians.
24.   1. 2. 3.
    1. Timothy.
25.   1. 2.
26.   3. 4.
27.   5. 6.
    2. Timothy.
28.   1. 2.
29.   3. 4.
    Titus.
30.   1. 2.
31.   3. and Philemon.
Iannary, Hebrewes.
1.   1. 2.
2.   3. 4.

of reading

3.	5. 6. 7.
4.	8. 9.
5.	10. 11.
6.	12. 13.

James.

| 7. | 1. 2. 3. |
| 8. | 4. 5. |

1. Peter.

| 9. | 1. 2. |
| 10. | 3. 4. 5. |

2. Peter.

| 11. | 1. 2. 3. |

1. John.

12.	1. 2. 3.
13.	4. 5.
14.	2. and 3. of John with Jude.

Revelation.

15.	1. 2. 3.
16.	4. 5. 6.
17.	7. 8. 9.
18.	10. 11. 12.
19.	13. 14. 15.
20.	16. 17. 18.

116 The order of the bookes and

21.	19. 20.
22.	21. 22.
	Psalmes.
23.	1.2.3.4 5.6.7.
24.	8.9.10.11.
25.	12.13.14.15.16.
26.	17.18.19.20.21.
27.	22.23.24.25.
28.	26.27.28.29.
29.	30.31.32.33.
30.	34.35.36.
31.	37.38.39.40.

February.

1.	41.42.43.44.
2.	45.46.47.48.
3.	49.50.51.
4.	52.53.54.55.56.
5.	57.58.59.60.
6.	61.62.63.64.
7.	65.66.67.
8.	68.69.
9.	70.71 72.
10.	73.74.75.76.
11.	77.78.

of reading the Scriptures.

12. 79. 80. 81.
13. 82. 83. 84. 85.
14. 86. 87. 88.
15. 89. 90.
16. 91. 92. 93. 94. 95.
17. 96. 97. 98. 99. 100.
18. 101. 102. 103.
19. 104. 105. 106.
20. 107. 108. 109. 110.
21. 111. 112. 113. 114. 115. 116. 117.
22. 118. 119. the halfe.
23. 119. the other halfe, 120. 121. 122.
24. 123. 124. 125. 126. 127. 128. 129.
25. 130. 131. 132. 133. 134. 135. 136.
26. 137. 138. 139. 140. 401. 142.
27. 143. 144. 145.
28. 146. 147. 148. 149. 150.

Rules

Rules or Titles of things to be obserued in reading.

Places that in reading I found sensible comfort in.

Places that in the reading of them I found did rebuke corruption in my nature or practise.

Places that shew the priuiledges of the godly aboue all other men.

Places that shew the affection I should beare to God.

Places that shew mee, how to cary my selfe in the Church.

Places that shew mee, how to cary my selfe in the family.

Promises that may comfort mee against the burthen of my daily infirmities.

Comforts against inward tentations and afflictions of spirit.

Promises to establish mee against the feare of falling away.

Promises that may comfort mee against outward crosses.

Grounds

ounds or places that shew mee
diuers points of religion, that I
could infallibly rest vpon & liue
and die in the assurance of them.
rd places that I would faine be
solued for the meaning of them,
mfortable places concerning
rayer.
ces that direct me in my particular calling.
ces that shew mee, how to cary
y selfe toward the wicked, espe-
ally when I must needes bee in
eir company.
mforts against death.
ces that shew the glory of heauen.
ces that set out the terror of
hell.
oice sentences to be learned
without booke.
tences for children to learne,
iefly expressing the chiefe
ints of religion.
ces against Hypocrisie.

The

The most memorable sayings of the godly in their seuerall estates.

Places that in reading I thinke might be wonderfull fit to comfort, or admonish, or direct such and such a friend.

Miscellanea or places I would faine remember, but I know not to what head to referre them.

RVLES of the second sort.

Places that iustifie our auoiding of worldly society with wicked men.

Places that iustifie a precise respect of the least sinne.

Places that concerne the strict keeping of the Sabboth.

Places that shew, that the godly haue stil bin reproched & slandered

Places that shew, that wee must be sorrow for our sinnes.

Places that shew, that the godly haue had all sorts of crosses.

Places that shew, that euen in the visible Church many times but a remnant shall be saued.

FINIS.

CPSIA information can be obtained at www.ICGtesting.com
Printed in the USA
LVOW02s0554100114

368851LV00008B/263/P